W9-AQV-632

Date: 2/3/12

**J 599.763 PET
Petrie, Kristin,
Kinkajous /**

PALM BEACH COUNTY
LIBRARY SYSTEM
3650 SUMMIT BLVD.
WEST PALM BEACH, FL 33406

Nocturnal Animals
Kinkajous

Kristin Petrie
ABDO Publishing Company

visit us at
www.abdopublishing.com

Published by ABDO Publishing Company, 8000 West 78th Street, Edina, Minnesota 55439.
Copyright © 2010 by Abdo Consulting Group, Inc. International copyrights reserved in all
countries. No part of this book may be reproduced in any form without written permission from the
publisher. The Checkerboard Library™ is a trademark and logo of ABDO Publishing Company.

Printed in the United States of America, North Mankato, Minnesota.
082009
012010

 PRINTED ON RECYCLED PAPER

Cover Photo: Peter Arnold
Interior Photos: Getty Images pp. 8, 10, 17, 21; National Geographic Image Collection pp. 1, 13, 19;
    Peter Arnold p. 16; Photo Researchers p. 7; Photolibrary pp. 5, 12, 15

Series Coordinator: Megan M. Gunderson
Editors: Heidi M.D. Elston, Megan M. Gunderson
Art Direction & Cover Design: Neil Klinepier

Library of Congress Cataloging-in-Publication Data

Petrie, Kristin, 1970-
  Kinkajous / Kristin Petrie.
     p. cm. -- (Nocturnal animals)
  Includes index.
  ISBN 978-1-60453-737-6
  1. Kinkajou--Juvenile literature. I. Title.
  QL737.C26P48 2010
  599.76'3--dc22
                  2009025654

Contents

Kinkajous 4

Fur and Feet 6

Forest Home 8

Busy Nights 10

Fruity Feasts 12

Growing Up 14

Hunted! 16

Human Threats 18

Save the Forests! 20

Glossary 22

Web Sites 23

Index 24

kinkajous

What creature sleeps all day, plays all night, and can have orange, glowing eyes? This animal can turn its feet around to run backward. And, it uses its furry tail like another arm!

This curious critter is the kinkajou. Are you still wondering what that is? Don't worry. Many people have never heard of this nocturnal animal. It lives high in the trees of certain forests. The kinkajou is rarely seen, but it is not rare.

The kinkajou is from the order Carnivora. Carnivores are a large group of mostly meat-eating animals. The order Carnivora includes the family **Procyonidae**. This is the kinkajou's family.

Within its family, the kinkajou is the only member of the genus *Potos*. The kinkajou's scientific name, *Potos flavus*, is Latin for "golden drinker." The golden-colored kinkajou is known for drinking nectar. Keep reading to learn more about this fascinating **arboreal** creature!

Nocturnal, Diurnal, or Crepuscular?

One way scientists group animals is by when they are most active. Nocturnal animals work and play during the night and sleep during the day. Diurnal animals are the opposite. They rest at night and are active during the day. Crepuscular animals are most active at twilight. This includes the time just before sunrise or just after sunset.

The kinkajou's fur is covered with an oily substance. Scientists believe this helps resist water.

Scientists use a method called scientific classification to sort organisms into groups. The basic classification system includes eight groups. In descending order, they are domain, kingdom, phylum, class, order, family, genus, and species.

Fur and Feet

This small creature weighs just 4.4 to 7 pounds (2 to 3.2 kg). The kinkajou's body is less than 24 inches (61 cm) long. Its tail adds another 16 to 22 inches (40 to 57 cm).

Soft, thick fur covers the kinkajou. It is either reddish brown or yellowish brown. The tail is often black tipped. The kinkajou's small, round face features large eyes and a short **muzzle**. Two low, rounded ears sit on its head.

This talented creature is built for living in trees. The kinkajou's front limbs end in **flexible** paws with short, sharp claws. They are perfect for climbing branches and grasping food.

The kinkajou's ankles and feet are also adapted for tree living. They can be turned backward! This helps the animal climb down trees headfirst.

The kinkajou's most notable feature is its **prehensile** tail. Like another arm, it grasps branches while the animal hangs upside down. It also helps the kinkajou maintain its balance. The kinkajou can even climb up its tail like a rope!

When reaching for something, a kinkajou may use its tail to hold on to a branch.

Forest Home

The kinkajou is native to southern Mexico, Central America, and parts of South America. Forested areas provide the kinkajou's number one need, trees. The kinkajou is **arboreal**. So it eats, sleeps, grooms, and plays high in the forest **canopy**. It rarely leaves the trees.

Frequently, a family of kinkajous shares a simple home. A family is usually made up of a female, two males, and two younger kinkajous.

Each family has its own territory, which the males defend. The territory's size is determined by the amount of food it can provide.

The males mark territory boundaries with scent markings. For this, they use scent glands near the mouth and on the throat and belly. Kinkajous also make a variety of sounds. These include threatening noises to guard their territory.

A kinkajou's home is usually a hole in a tree.

N
W · E
S

GREENLAND

NORTH
AMERICA

EUROPE

ASIA

AFRICA

SOUTH
AMERICA

AUSTRALIA

Where Kinkajous Live

Mexico

Belize

Honduras

Guatemala

Nicaragua

El Salvador

Guyana

Suriname

Venezuela

Costa Rica

French
Guiana

Colombia

Panama

Ecuador

Peru

Brazil

Bolivia

DETAIL RANGE MAP

Busy Nights

The kinkajou is nicknamed "nightwalker."

Kinkajous are nocturnal animals. In the warm daytime hours, these animals sleep. But at sunset, they get to work!

What does a kinkajou do all night? It starts with grooming and socializing. After this, the hungry kinkajou begins its solitary search for food. Other activities include protecting its home. Usually, the kinkajou travels the same route each night. In the morning, it returns home to sleep.

How do kinkajous carry out these activities in the dark? Their large eyes are well equipped to take in as much light as possible. That makes the dark a little less dark!

Nocturnal Eyes

Some lucky nocturnal animals have special eye features that help them in the dark. They may have large eyes compared to their body size. Also, their pupils may open wider than ours do in low light. These two features allow more light to enter their eyes.

After light enters an eye's pupil, the lens focuses it on the retina. In the retina, two special kinds of cells receive the light. These are rods and cones.

Rods work in low light. They detect size, shape, and brightness. Cones work in bright light. They detect color and details. Nocturnal animals often have many more rods than cones.

Many nocturnal eyes also have a tapetum lucidum behind the retina. The tapetum is like a mirror. Light bounces off of it and back through the retina a second time. This gives the light another chance to strike the rods. The reflected light then continues back out through the pupil. This causes the glowing eyes you may see at night!

NIGHT ANIMAL

DAY ANIMAL

RETINA

RODS

CONES

RETINA

TAPETUM LUCIDUM

RETINA

LENS

PUPIL

ANIMAL'S EYE (side view)

Fruity Feasts

The kinkajou may belong to the order Carnivora, but it is actually an omnivore. In fact, the kinkajou tends to eat more plants than animals.

The kinkajou feasts on many types of fruit. The selection depends on what is in season. Figs make up a large portion of the kinkajou's diet. They are available all year long.

Plants add to the kinkajou's diet. Leaves and flowers make a nice lunch. Nectar and honey are sweet treats.

Kinkajous stick their long tongues into flowers. This gets pollen on their faces (right page). The pollen transfers to the next plant they eat, which helps the forest grow!

The kinkajou uses its skinny, five-inch (13-cm) tongue to slurp them up! This habit may explain one of the kinkajou's nicknames, "honey bear."

A hungry kinkajou's diet may also include insects. Ants and termites make crunchy snacks. The kinkajou may also eat eggs, small mammals, and birds. It holds food in one hand to eat. Frequently, it hangs upside down while enjoying its meal!

Growing Up

A kinkajou's life begins with the mating of a family's female and one male. Females can begin reproducing at age two and a quarter. Males can reproduce when they are one and a half years old.

A female kinkajou usually carries one young at a time for 112 to 118 days. Rarely, she gives birth to two young at once. The kinkajou is born in a hollow tree. It weighs five to seven ounces (150 to 200 g) at birth. Blind and helpless, it requires its mother's full attention.

By two months old, the young kinkajou is eating solid food. And, it can already hang by its tail! At three or four months old, it begins learning to search for its own food.

The mother kinkajou nurses her young until it is about four months old. At age two and a half, a female leaves her family group. Males remain in the group. They frequently form strong bonds. And, territories pass from father to son.

The kinkajou is thought to live an average of 19 years. Yet in **captivity**, one lived to age 40!

When resting, females hold their young to their chests. While climbing, they will carry their young in their mouths.

Hunted!

The jaguar's name comes from a word meaning "he who kills with one leap."

The kinkajou appears to live a good life. It eats and plays all night and sleeps all day. Its nocturnal habits keep it out of sight from many predators. Its **arboreal** life protects it from many land-loving enemies.

Yet, a daytime nap in the trees still has its risks. The kinkajou has several natural predators. From above, birds such as the harpy eagle and Isidor's eagle search for sleeping kinkajous. At night, other predators prowl from below. Wildcats such as the jaguar and the ocelot may pounce quickly on the kinkajou.

When attacked, kinkajous fight back. They grasp predators with their limbs. This includes their strong tails! And, they use their sharp teeth to bite back.

Kinkajous can turn their feet completely around and run quickly in both directions. This helps them escape predators!

Human Threats

The kinkajou has few natural predators. However, it faces many challenges from humans. Humans hunt and capture the kinkajou for several reasons. Some locals enjoy kinkajou meat. People also export the meat to other countries.

Humans hunt the kinkajou for its **pelt**, too. The little creature's velvety coat is valuable in the fur trade. In addition, humans capture and sell kinkajous as pets. Yet kinkajous do not make good pets. They have a dangerous, painful bite. And, they can damage a home at night when they are most active.

Loss of **habitat** is another challenge the kinkajou faces. Most habitat loss is due to **deforestation**. Deforestation forces animals to share smaller areas of their natural habitat. This creates overcrowding and food shortages. What little forest is left cannot support the animals. With too little food and space, entire animal populations may die.

Save the Forests!

The kinkajou's future looks bright. Although rarely seen, kinkajou populations are believed to be strong. Scientists are not concerned that the kinkajou will become extinct.

Still, this animal and its **habitat** must be protected. People must prevent overhunting. This will keep too many kinkajous from being killed for their meat and fur. Also, limitations on their capture and sale are needed.

Forest preservation is just as vital. Many organizations are already working to protect the forests of Central and South America. These **conservation** efforts will benefit the kinkajou and its neighbors.

Luckily, the kinkajou lives in many of these protected areas. With careful awareness, this fascinating creature's population will remain strong!

Scientists are learning more about kinkajous by studying them in their natural habitat.

Glossary

arboreal (ahr-BAWR-ee-uhl) - living in or frequenting trees.

canopy - the uppermost spreading, branchy layer of a forest.

captivity - the state of being captured and held against one's will.

conservation - the planned management of natural resources to protect them from damage or destruction.

deforestation - the act of removing trees and clearing forests.

flexible - able to bend or move easily.

habitat - a place where a living thing is naturally found.

muzzle - an animal's nose and jaws.

pelt - an animal skin with the fur still attached.

prehensile - adapted for grasping or holding. Some monkeys and other animals have prehensile tails.

Procyonidae (proh-see-AHN-uh-dee) - the scientific name for the raccoon family. Members of this family are called procyonids. They include raccoons, coatis, and kinkajous.

Web Sites

To learn more about kinkajous, visit ABDO Publishing Company on the World Wide Web at **www.abdopublishing.com**. Web sites about kinkajous are featured on our Book Links page. These links are routinely monitored and updated to provide the most current information available.

Index

B
body 6, 8

C
captivity 14, 20
Carnivora (order) 4, 12
Central America 8, 20
classification 4
claws 6
coat 6, 18, 20
color 4, 6
communication 8
conservation 20

D
defense 8, 10, 16, 17
deforestation 18
diet 4, 6, 8, 10, 12, 13, 14, 16, 18

E
ears 6
enemies 16, 17, 18
eyes 4, 6, 10

F
feet 4, 6

G
grooming 8, 10

H
habitat 4, 6, 8, 14, 16, 17, 18, 20
head 6
homes 8, 10
hunting 10, 14

L
life cycle 14
life span 14

M
Mexico 8
muzzle 6, 8

P
pets 18
playing 4, 8, 16
Potos (genus) 4
Procyonidae (family) 4

R
reproduction 14

S
scent glands 8
scent marking 8
senses 10, 14
size 6, 13, 14
sleeping 4, 8, 10, 16, 17
socializing 10
South America 8, 20

T
tail 4, 6, 14, 17
teeth 17
territory 8, 14
tongue 13

Y
young 8, 14